POSH FROCKS AND POSTINGS

Posh Frocks and Postings

A Second Collection of Poems
written by Maggie May

"One thing a man seems to hate doing
Is passing those notes from the Mess
Addressed to his wife, about parties or drinks,
For he fears that she'll want a new dress!"

Illustrated by
Al Turner

Typeset by DP Photosetting, Aylesbury, Bucks
Printed and bound in Great Britain by
BPC Hazell Books Ltd
Aylesbury, Bucks, England
Member of BPC Ltd

FOR FRANCES

who has been an inspiration
during the writing of this book

Contents

Introduction

When I finished writing WAITING IN THE WINGS, my first book about RAF wives, I thought I had covered all the situations that confront us long-suffering ladies. But in the few years since then, I have remembered, sighed over and laughed at, many more which have come tumbling into this second volume of poems.

So here is the air force wife in POSH FROCKS AND POSTINGS, once again coping with further adventures of the dining-in nights, Wives Club committees, boarding school . . . and the circumstances of the recent Gulf war. All of these sad, funny and frustrating situations can happen to every one of us, regardless of our husband's rank, branch or trade.

The second half of the collection takes our lives a stage further and presents a view of that unenviable role . . . the Station Commander's wife, whose high-flying position is perhaps the greatest test for an RAF wife's sense of humour. Constantly in the spotlight, she is expected to host VIPs, dazzle at dinner parties and prop up other wives in trouble.

Her home (the Des Res) is used by all and run by the Treasure. Being "Mrs Staish", as she is often called, is a mixture of First Lady, Agony Aunt and Hostess of the Year. It can be exhilarating, exhausting, thankless – but never dull.

My thanks are due to Al Turner who has once again illustrated the book in his inimitable style and humour, and to my husband John who provided me with the opportunity for being a Station Commander's wife at RAF Binbrook. I hope the poems will continue to inspire and entertain air force wives everywhere.

Maggie May

Foreword

From Air Chief Marshal Sir Thomas Kennedy GCB AFC DL

Maggie May's first book "Waiting in the Wings" was an instant success. The proceeds went to the Benevolent Fund's Reach for the Sky Appeal and made a significant contribution towards the target which, with your help was achieved. The book seemed to strike a chord within its readers that brought back memories of occasions and experiences ranging across the entire spectrum of human emotions. Some were great fun, some were sad, many were interesting, many were dead boring, a lot of them were absolutely infuriating. What about the ones that were, frustrating, embarrassing, successful, disastrous, hilarious, or washed out? And the ones that are best forgotten?

This second volume will enable you to laugh about them once again. All those moments that are so clearly registered in the mind and which can be recalled over a drink "I remember when we were . . .". Good on you Maggie, keep up the good work. And to you dear reader, thank you for the support you are giving once again to the Fund.

Controller
Royal Air Force Benevolent Fund

A Bluey To The Gulf

I've just had your lovely long letter
And thought I'd write back straight away –
Let's hope that this war is soon over
And you can come back to UK,

It seems such an age since you left, Love,
Although it's been just a few weeks,
And I'm trying so hard to keep cheerful
But some days life seems a bit bleak;

I try not to think of the danger
But glad that the heat's not too bad,
Are they giving you plenty to eat, Dear?
Lack of beer must be driving you mad!

Things are all right, could be better,
The kids miss their dad you can guess,
They've both got bad coughs and can't settle
And the house is a permanent mess,

The men came to fit that new carpet
So *that* was a day full of fun,
They took out the old one and slung it
. . . Then found that they'd sent the wrong one!

Barrack Stores *promised* they'd sort it
(It's over two days since they came)
But wives never get the same treatment
As husbands – they should be *ashamed*!

I don't half feel lonely without you
This time it's much worse than before –
It's daft, but I felt quite nostalgic
At the sight of your socks . . . on the floor,

Take care in that dangerous desert
(I bet you are *sick* of the sand)
Some days I hate what you're doing
But mostly I do understand:

The quarter seems empty without you
(But those socks make me feel you are near!)
And I'm counting the days till you're home, Love,
For it isn't half lonely back here.

Transports Of Delight

We've moved many times for the air force
But this move was worse than the rest
– It was pouring with rain, they came *two hours* late
(So my humour was put to the test)

When the three of them stood on the doorstep,
I couldn't believe my own eyes . . .
There was one "geriatric", one big burly Scot,
And a chap who was clearly "pint-size"!

There was one 'geriatric', one big burly Scot
and a chap who was clearly 'pint size'

There could only be one explanation,
I felt, for this odd-looking crew,
We'd been set up for one of those shows on TV
And the cameras would soon be in view . . .

But, alas, it was no such good fortune!
With blankets and crates from the van
They proceeded to pack our possessions forthwith
(And I feared things would not go to plan)

The old chap, called Alf, had been poorly
So wasn't quite up to the task,
The Scotsman, called Jock, was a "brickie" by trade
. . . Could they *cope*? (but I didn't dare ask)

Charlie (the pint-size) was humping
A massive crate packed full of books
(He surely would buckle beneath all that weight?
But he's stronger, it seems, than he looks)

The whole day was just like a nightmare,
With pouring rain, wet feet and all,
And I seemed to do nothing but make cups of tea
As the chaps dashed about in the hall . . .

I heard something "go" on the landing
(The wardrobe was wedged on the stair)
Then I spotted them dragging a table along
"That thing's fragile!" I yelled, "have a care. . ."

The hours ticked by, we became frantic
– They'd stripped every *inch* of the place
But just as they brought the last load downstairs
. . . They found that they'd run out of space.

Another van had to be sent for
(These problems do happen, we know)
But *why* don't things get any *better*
Each time that we pack up and go?

Thrift Shop Fever

It's Thursday at the Thrift Shop
And the queue is mounting fast
At Opening Time they rush in
With a gleam as they storm past . . .

A gallant band of helpers
At tables, poised we sit,
Spotting this week's bargains
(And hoping they will fit!)

We get all kinds of items
And book them in with glee
For someone else's cast-off
Could be just our "cup of tea"

The tickets, stamped and ready,
Adorn each hopeful sale,
And as we tag each garment
Ouch – another broken nail!

Not a hope of selling

16

This lady is determined
To demand the highest price
(– A pity, for the truth is
Her goods aren't very nice)

An out-of-fashion kaftan
And skirt in leopard skin
Have not a *hope* of selling
But she boldly puts them in:

Now here's a good selection
From a lady who has flair
(Half these won't reach the hangers
We'll just drape them on our chair)

A little Jaeger number!
Just the thing for next week's do,
We fight to see who gets it,
There's a matching handbag too –

And what about this ballgown?
Can't let it go, that's clear,
With all these clothes to tempt us
It's *expensive*, working here!

Once, we'd never dream of
Buying things that weren't brand new
But now we often do it
(And we look so well-dressed, too)

The rails have clothes from Harrods
Hanging next to C and A's,
And they've one thing in common
. . . They've all seen better days:

So next time you go shopping
And in favourite shop you drift,
Just think – that dress you're buying
Could end up in the Thrift!

"I've forgotten what a Christmas NOT spent on a beach is like"

Letter From Sunny Climes

Dear All, this Christmas letter
Is the last one you will get
That's written on this sunny beach
. . . I'm feeling quite upset,

We've just heard we are posted
Back to jolly old UK
To somewhere in the sticks, of course,
(It's really made my day)

Do hope you're well and cheerful
At this festive time of year
(It's hard to think of Christmas pud
In all the heat out here)

I've forgotten what a Christmas
Not spent on a beach is like
– All that wrestling with the turkey
. . . I think I'll go on strike!

The thought of all the packing
And the dreaded march out too
Plus leaving all this sunshine,
I feel ghastly – wouldn't you?

No more trips and "duty frees"
No maids to help me out,
Instead, it's back to wind and rain
That's what it's all about:

It's *such* a change from England
When you're living Overseas
– No rush hour, fog, or frozen pipes
No queues at Sainsbury's . . .

For us, blue skies and water sports
Are what we're used to now,
So wearing vests and woolly tights
Will be a shock somehow!

It's really going to hit us
And we'll miss the LOA,
Goodbye to all this high life
When we're back in the UK,

Just think – this time next Christmas
We'll be harassed, tired and broke,
But one thing we'll be sure of,
We'll be back with all you folk:

With Mum and Dad and Auntie Vi
And dear old cousin Jack
Three Christmases without you all
(It's high time we came back)

Who needs idyllic settings,
White sands and palms that sway?
Who wouldn't swap the lot
To be back home . . . in the UK!

The Posh Frock

How often does it happen
When you pop to the Boutique,
You spot a little Number
But your conscience starts to tweak?

You try to walk straight past it
But you feel it's really *you*,
Besides, it's what you're *needing*
To wear to Friday's do . . .

The salesgirl spots you looking
(You *know* you shouldn't buy it)
Too late, she's swooped upon you
Saying "Would you care to try it?"

A second's hesitation
Then to fitting room you go
(It's "communal" and heaving
And undies . . . overflow)

Someone's doing battle
With zip that doesn't meet
It's "bottoms up" – arms flying
(Not to mention all that heat)

You peel off outer garments
Then dive in, like the rest,
You hope the outfit's worth it
And will make you feel well-dressed.

That first glance in the mirror
Tells you . . . this is really *it*,
(You'll trim the household budget
No smoked salmon for a bit!)

When husband sees you in it
And admiring kiss he plonks,
Just smile, then sweetly tell him –
"Oh *this*? . . . I've had it *yonks*!"

The Morning After

I take it you had a good evening?
– You staggered to bed about four,
And you said "what a *great* dining-in night"
(I think I've heard *that* one before)

I must say, you don't look too hot, Dear

I wasn't amused when you woke me,
You fell in a heap on the bed!
You've forgotten you slept in your braces?
. . . What a *shame* you have such a bad head:

I must say, you don't look too hot, Dear,
– Did you sup the odd pint of beer?
I think I'll just open the window
(It reeks like a brewery in here!)

I've brought you a nice steaming cuppa
Yes, I must be a wonderful wife,
And thank God for a good sense of humour,
I need it in this crazy life . . .

So the chaps burned that broken piano?
And you all fell about at that stage?
Yes, I know it's an air force tradition
But when will you chaps act your *age*?

I did think, as men became older
They were meant to grow up, just a bit,
But at Guest Nights you act just like youngsters,
So things never change, I'll admit . . .

You ask will I please treat you gently?
That you need to be pampered today,
And was I aware I was *shouting*?
And you'd just like some toast on a tray . . .

I'll remind you that when you get up, Dear,
I've got several jobs you can do
– Oh don't tell me . . . you're having a *relapse*
And can't do a thing – so what's new?

23

I Am Only A Wife

Now this has been one of those terrible days,
And my husband's away once again,
The pipes are all frozen, four light bulbs have blown,
So I'm having a moan . . . about *men*!

My pipes weren't his major concern . . .

It's super for him being out in the sun
But not very jolly back here,
We're snowed in, no milk, and the Naafi's cut off
And *when* will the plumber appear?

I rang up the Office, reporting my pipes
Stating: "I am a wife on my own",
But where was the sympathy, help or advice?
All I got was this voice, like a stone:

The chap took my message, unmoved I could tell,
My pipes weren't his major concern,
I am only a wife, just one more on his list
(You'd think that by now I would learn)

And so, hopping mad, I stormed off on foot
To tackle this chap face to face,
How *dare* they talk down to us, time after time,
And how would *they* feel in our place?

He visibly wilted on hearing my tale
(And seemed lost for words, I could tell)
He didn't expect to be shot down in flames
For wives aren't supposed to rebel:

Hours later, still frozen, no plumber's appeared
And I *long* for the sight of his van,
But one thing's for sure, the next time around
– I'm going to come back . . . as a man!

Going Crackers At Christmas

I'm trying so hard to feel festive
And get in a bright Christmas mood
But all I am in is a *panic*
Surrounded by mountains of food!

The turkey weighs more than I wanted
How long does it need? I don't know,
And the stuffing and mince pies aren't done yet
(I wish I could let it all *go*)

So I ask you – what is it all FOR?

The mistletoe's up, and the holly,
And I've made a cone wreath for the door
But I see that the wind's blown it over
So I ask you – what is it all *for*?

I've battled in shops for the presents,
Bought trinkets and things for the tree,
Now I'm feeling too tired to enjoy it
– Why is every darned thing left to *me*?

I'll pour out a tot of this brandy
To give the old pudding a treat
And I'll have one myself, while I'm at it
(It might help my poor aching feet)

All this effort is driving me crackers,
My 'snap' has all gone, that's for sure!
And my 'motto' is: Rally Round Mother
Before I collapse on the floor . . .

My husband's come home looking cheerful
And asks why I look fraught, and "all in" –
"It's all under control . . . nothing to it,
So why panic?" he says with a grin;

Does he think all this happens by magic?
He has no *idea* what I've done!
It must be so nice to just stroll in
And say . . . "Isn't Christmas . . . *fun*?"

So I'll sort out this gigantic turkey
(When it's crammed in the oven I'll cheer)
And the best thing of all about Christmas?
– It only comes round once a year!

Over The Garden Fence

It's been a week, I tell you,
When I nearly blew my top,
It started with the Exercise,
And since then . . . just non-stop:

Would other wives believe it,
What we air force wives go through?
The postings and the beer calls,
And the long detachments too . . .

And what about the march out –
Why *do* we all go through it?
That scrubbing round the windows!
(We must be *mad* to do it)

'If it doesn't move, they'll paint it –'

28

Have you had the painters yet?
Well, don't get your hopes too high,
When they finished here last Thursday
I sat and had a cry,

I knew they weren't the brightest
(For I've seen them here before)
But they *painted round* the raincoat
That was hanging on the door!

Don't laugh, you're next, they told me
(But believe *that*, if you like)
If it doesn't move, they'll paint it
– We should tell them "On your bike" . . .

And what about the Guest Night?
Were you woken up, like me?
So yours slept in the hallway?
– Mine collapsed at half past three!

Men never change, God bless them,
We should know the score by now,
But when you're soft and gullible
You live in hope, somehow . . .

It looks like mine's come home now,
Wanting supper on the dot –
Of all the things we cope with
I think husbands . . . top the lot!

This valiant band of helpers

Wives Club Fayre

The Wives Club Fayre Committee
Were deciding what to do
To raise some funds this Christmas
And think of something *new*:

With heavy sighs and scratching heads
(And cups of tea galore)
They all concluded – this year's fayre
Would be like those before!

The Raffle and Tombola
And Handicrafts and Cakes
Would need a lot of helping hands
(Their knees began to quake)

The Secretary tries to get
Some volunteers for teas,
The Chairman, looking desperate,
Says: "Come on ladies . . . *please!*"

Someone mentions sausage rolls
And squabbles soon arise,
How many? and who'll cook them?
And what about the *size*?

An over-powering lady
(Who thinks she has a flair)
Takes over the debate, and cries:
"*I'll* cook them all, so there!"

Some frantic days then followed
Of knits and bakes and brews,
Collecting tins and stitching bags
And gathering in the booze:

The helpers on the Handicrafts
Were swamped with strange delights,
Like ghastly purple place mats
That were made from knitted tights!

One wife's jars of chutney
Were the best, she had no doubt
(The contest now was hotting up
And wives were falling out)

The Wives Club Fayre Committee
Stopped at *nothing* to ensure
That funds would hit the jackpot
And outdo all Fayres before . . .

Husbands were neglected
As wives "got into gear"
– Around the patch the air was blue
As Christmas Fayre drew near,

The wives could talk of nothing else
And husbands had a moan
"They cook all day – but *not for us*,
– They're always on the *'phone*!"

The day then dawned, and willing wives
Set up the wretched fete,
With pulses racing, faces flushed,
All in a nervous state:

The ladies on Refreshment Stall,
Poised to quench each thirst,
Had sausage rolls set neatly out
For those who got there first,

At two o'clock they *flooded* in,
(A quite amazing sight)
The sausage rolls were hoovered up
By all who had a bite,

White Elephants . . . the Potted Plants . . .
Folk couldn't get *enough*!
And even on the Handicrafts
They sold the strangest stuff,

This valiant band of helpers
With a mystifying power
Had done what none had done before
– Sold out, within the hour:

The ladies now were shattered,
Their feet were throbbing too,
But oh the glory of it
Was *worth* what they'd gone through . . .

The Wives Club Fayre Committee,
Quite wrung out with Christmas cheer,
Said: "If they want another one
– Find someone else, next year!"

Boarding School Blues

Dear Mum and Dad
I hope you are well
– I wish I could say I'm all right
But it feels like a prison here,
Really it does
And I cry in my pillow at night . . .

If you could see
What they give us for lunch
You would *gasp* at the sight of the stuff,
Revolting rice puddings
And stew all the time
I tell you – I've just had *enough*.

"I tell you – I've just had ENOUGH!"

Don't make me stay here
I've had this bad head,
And terrible eye ache as well!
I can't sleep at night
For the noise in the dorm
This place, in a word, is *hell*:

Oh *please* can I leave?
I'm not feeling well,
I've got a quite horrible cough . . .
The Head is so strict
And he's twisted his foot
(I wish his whole leg had come off!)

I bet when you read this
You'll toss it aside
And think that I soon will feel better;
Excuse the smudged ink
It's . . . only . . . my tears
As I write you this heart-rending letter!

I know how you like
To hear all my news
(Most days I'm feeling quite *sick*)
Must close now
It's tea
(Bet it's corned beef *again*)
Please write soon
From your homesick son,
Nick.

The Wife Who Waits

On the settee a remarkable lady
Sits pensive, unflustered, as calm as can be
While news of the war was unfolding before us
Brought into the room, on lunchtime TV

Her husband is out there, amid all the fighting
But staunchly her gaze never strays from the screen;
Her thoughts, if in turmoil, so carefully hidden –
She laughingly chatters to lighten the scene

We talk of the danger and watch the news broadcast
– Two aircrew have landed from bombing Iraq . . .
From so far away, yet now standing before us!
They'd gone on their mission and safely come back

Her husband, well-trained in professional combat,
Has practised for war (as our men have to do)
A wife has no drill, no procedures to follow
– It's all about coping, and seeing it through

We switch off TV and discuss all the problems,
She's full of concern for the mothers and wives
Who've had to face up to their men's sudden absence,
Who've not known a parting before in their lives

This wife showed her strength, and great sense of humour
(As much as this war situation allowed)
For, just like her husband, she's part of the battle
. . . And if he could see how she copes, he'd be proud.

(Thursday 17th January 1991)

37

And now the role of
Station Commander's Wife . . .

"So I'll take a deep breath in this elegant house
As I start this exciting new life
And pray I can cope, in this very Des Res
With my role as the CO's wife . . ."

I had 'called' as we did in those days

Mrs Staish

When I first heard about his promotion
And how we were coming up here
On a tour as a *station commander*
I was gripped by this feeling of fear!

It wasn't a prospect I relished,
Becoming the new CO's wife,
So I sought the true wisdom and guidance
Of others who'd coped with this life . . .

They told me some hair-raising stories,
Some cheered me with good common sense,
But until you have actually *started*,
You simply can't help feeling tense,

I remembered a lady from way back
Who had been in the same situation,
She was frightfully snooty and distant
And swept, full of pomp, round the station:

As a young naive wife, newly married,
I had "called" as we did in those days,
She looked down her nose as she offered me tea
And I vowed not to follow *her* ways!

Thank Heavens that custom is over,
No wife will go through that with me!
I like to make people feel *welcome*
Whenever I offer them tea . . .

They tell me there's nothing to beat it,
(At this moment I'm quite overcome)
The new "Mrs Staish" is about to arrive
Are they ready for this? – here I come!

*Just the right amount
To get them nicely merry . . .*

The Treasure

I couldn't quite imagine
How my life would be
Living in the Residence
'Midst all the luxury –
Those *fifty seven* doorknobs
And eleven sinks throughout!
(Thank heavens there's a "Treasure"
To come and help me out . . .)

This staunch and loyal lady
Is a must for wives like me
Who have to cope with visitors
And endless cups of tea,
For sometimes I must dash off
To a welfare case or two
But while I'm out, my Treasure
Will have cleaned the house right through:

She's a dab hand with the Hoover
(It drones . . . incessantly!)
And she whistles while she's working
For she's cheerful as can be,
Her arms look *made* for polishing
At scrubbing she's a peach,
The sinks and loos are gleaming
(But we get through *stacks* of bleach)

She wears a frilly apron
When ladies come for sherry
And pours them just the right amount
To get them nicely merry . . .
She helps at dinner parties,
Likes a healthy appetite,
So piles the plates with extra veg
(The guests can't move all night!)

She tackles mounds of ironing
With the iron set rather hot
The odd thing has a scorch mark
(Which she hopes that I won't spot!)
She's been here for so long now,
Works her fingers to the bone
I'm inclined to think that *she*'s in charge
The house is like her own . . .

Yes, living in the Residence
Can be a laugh, it's true,
For often when the phone rings
She calls: "Eh oop . . . it's *for you!*"
Her job is very varied,
She's so many parts to play,
A cleaner, steward, laundry maid
– She does them all, her way:

It sounds a life of 'Riley'
But I have to say – it's not!
I sometimes long to be alone
In some more tranquil spot,
To flee the dreaded Hoover
And the visitors that call
For even with a Treasure
. . . You just can't win 'em all.

Who'd Be A CO's Wife?

One day Mrs Staish had a problem
She was faced with an unpleasant task
(There was only one wife who could do it
But she didn't know *quite* how to ask . . .)

So she took the unfortunate lady
That morning, to shop in the town
Trying hard to be carefree and jolly
But scarcely suppressing a frown:

If only she knew the right moment –
Should they stop for a coffee or two?
But the shop was packed out and she panicked
That her friend might walk out (wouldn't you?)

When they returned with their shopping
Mrs Staish asked her friend to pop in,
For they'd not had the chance of a natter
– How about a nice sherry or gin?

In the lounge was a workman . . . and chaos,
(Fate was working against her somehow)
So her friend said: "Let's leave it, you're busy"
Mrs Staish thought "It's got to be *now!*"

She sat the poor soul in the kitchen
Said: "I'd just like a word in your ear . . ."
Her friend gasped – "You're going to ask me
To take on the wives club . . . Oh dear!"

A Dash To The Naafi

I've had to pop into the Naafi
(I needed a quarter of ham)
How I wish I could sneak in, unnoticed,
So people won't know who I am . . .

For the problem about this position
Is being "on show" so to speak,
The Image is vital, wherever you go,
For they notice a smudge on your cheek!

But I thought in a place like the Naafi
(Not known for its "get up and go")
I could slide, with no fuss, through the checkout
. . . But they've spotted it's me, what a blow:

I feel I have failed expectations

46

Did I put on some lipstick this morning?
(I daren't even *look* at my hair)
There's a hole in these tights, getting bigger,
And they've all stopped to chat! It's not fair,

They take in my "total ensemble"
– The lot, as they give me the eye,
And I feel I have failed expectations
(Is this what they call "flying high"?)

The Manager comes up to greet me
(A persistent but affable type)
"We've a new line in pies, can I show you?
And our Produce is lovely and ripe . . ."

He proudly shows off the six carrots
And five wilting leeks on display,
With a twinkle he asks: "Can I tempt you?"
And I hastily cry: "Not today!"

I've found yet *another* dilemma
That everyone notes what you buy!
It's so hard to escape with one packet of ham
(They're expecting your bill to be high)

Eyes watch as I slink to the checkout
(I can just *feel* that hole in my tights)
But there *must* be a way of surviving
When you're flying at such dizzy heights!

A pity we can't have a cuddle or two

The Back Seat

The staff car and driver are waiting outside
To whisk us in style to the do,
The driver salutes as he opens the door
And I sink in the back, Dear, with you:

I feel like the Queen, it's exciting and new,
And I fold my legs slowly and smile:
What fun going off in this elegant way
And shall we hold hands for a while?

The last time we sat on a back seat together
Was when we were kids, long ago –
Who would have thought we'd be sitting like this?
(No wonder my cheeks are aglow)

I won't have to drive us both home, as I do,
What a wonderful perk of this life!
I'm changing my mind – it's not bad after all
To be the new CO's wife . . .

The driver sits calmly up there in the front
(He can hear every *word* that we say)
But if we don't speak he'll think "what a dull pair"
So it seems we can't win either way:

It's a pity we can't have a cuddle or two
(Sometimes being CO is a *pain*)
But you're looking remote . . . not reckless like me
And you're saying, you're sure it will rain,

I'll soon be quite used to this riding around
(Just a matter of getting the knack)
But no-one would guess at the thoughts in my head
When I'm sitting with you in the back!

Swap The Gloves And Handbag

When your husband is the CO of the station
And as his wife you share the limelight too,
At times it can be utterly confusing
With all the situations you go through . . .

*You swap the gloves and handbag
for the plasters*

You often have to pay a welfare visit
To a wife in trouble and distress,
You get home, clutching gloves and matching handbag,
To find . . . a bleeding knee that's in a mess!

Yes, you swap the gloves and handbag for the plasters
As soon as you have staggered through the door,
One minute, you're an unpaid social worker
The next – you're just a mother as before.

Those committees where you're made to feel important
Taking big decisions on the spot,
Still leave you in a dither over supper,
Should you cook a chicken, chops . . . or what?

You're driven in a staff car to receptions
And feel about as pampered as can be,
Next day, swap gloves and handbag for the trolley,
As you're shopping you think: which role's really *me*?

You meet and greet the wives at sherry mornings
(And they're eyeing up each item that you wear)
But later, swap your gladrags for the apron
(In slippers you've not *quite* such style and flair . . .)

Presiding over lunches, making speeches,
Is something else you cope with on the way,
But at least they listen, rapt, to what you're saying!
(At home they never hear a word you say)

With all this socialising thrust upon you
You need domestic staff to help you out,
And it's bliss, all week, to never hold a duster
– Your "Treasure" sees the house is clean throughout;

On Saturdays you're thankful for a breather
From all those hectic functions in your life,
So you swap the gloves and handbag for . . . the *hoover*
– At weekends, you are just another wife!

*I couldn't but notice the difference in how I'd
been treated before . . .*

Special Delivery

We all know what wives in the air force
Endure in the ordinary way,
But things change when you're given a "status"
And it's rather a shock, I must say:

For a funny thing happened this morning
When I found that our light bulbs were low
– It was clear that to Barrack Stores, pronto,
Was where I now needed to go,

As I walked in, they almost *saluted*!
And asked: would I care for a seat?
When I told them I just needed light bulbs
Some *extra* chaps leapt to their feet:

Now, we all know the *usual* reception
Wives get as we walk through the door,
So I couldn't but notice the difference
From how I'd been treated before . . .

I had to restrain a few giggles
Especially when one of them said,
"We'd not *dream* of you carrying light bulbs
So we'll send our van with them, instead,"

In a flash, I thought back to a moment
Of twelve years ago, maybe more,
As young mum with toddler in pushchair
I had gone to the same Barrack Store

I'd struggled back home with some saucepans
On foot, for I'd no car that day,
Now *that*'s when wives need some attention
. . . Much more than on days like today!

VIP Visit

The Commander in Chief and his lady
Are coming up here for the day
– I haven't a clue how I'll manage
So I'll just have to do it . . . my way,

My husband will host the Air Marshal
While I must look after his wife,
To offer her sherry and show her around
And chat about RAF life:

I'll have to get out the best gladrags
(I bet that I won't sleep *that* night)
Our first VIPs! I must try to relax
And trust it will work out all right . . .

Their car has drawn up in the driveway
(I am feeling quite sick, suddenly)
The men disappear, Lady L comes inside
For (you've guessed it) a nice cup of tea!

Back at the Residence, later

Some of the wives have now joined us
To give me some moral support
They're laughing and cheerful (thank heavens for that)
And not like me – harassed and fraught:

My Treasure is poised with the tea tray
(She's coping so far very well)
But I'm praying she won't drop a "clanger" today
And let out: "Eh oop Lady L!"

It's time to go off in the staff car
To visit some clubs on the Station
(She's rather reserved so it's left up to me
To engage her in light conversation)

I show her the Mothers and Toddlers,
The Creche where the children can play,
Lady L loves the kids but my eye's on the clock
So it's hard when I drag her away . . .

Lunch is laid on for the ladies
At the Officers' Mess, what a treat,
Lady L is relaxed, tells me over the wine
That she suffers a lot with her feet!

I suddenly feel so much better,
She is human, like all of the rest –
No need for the nerves, she had been through it too
She says "be yourself is the best"

Back at the Residence, later,
Lady L and I kick off our shoes,
We have to admit . . . it's one hell of a day
When you cope with these VIP dos!

Barry In The Des Res

I've just met the new lady
Who's the wife of the CO,
She's absolutely *dotty*
About Barry Manilow!

Raving about Barry just might help my career!

She says she has his poster
Hanging on her kitchen wall
And hopes we'll play his records
At next month's Summer Ball:

She told me she loves discos
When they hold them in the Mess,
And asked me if I like to dance,
I gulped and said: "Er . . . yes . . ."

I heard my mates all laughing
As they sat there in the crowd
And hearing Barry warbling
Made me want to groan out loud –

She *loved* my pale pink sweater,
Told me Barry's is the same!
(I suppose I should be *flattered*
At this dubious claim to fame . . .)

I swear she started *swooning*
So I felt I had no choice,
I swung her round the floor a bit,
Remarking on his voice,

I said I liked his music
(No flies on me, no fear,
For raving about Barry
Just might help my career!)

To chat with CO's ladies
Can be difficult, you know,
But now – we'll all be *grateful*
. . . To Barry Manilow!

Dinner With The Locals

It's kind of you both to invite us
To come to your dinner tonight,
No, I don't know a thing about Farming
But I'm sure you will soon put me right!

Yes, we've been here for six weeks already
And I'm finding there's plenty to do,
It's a new world for me, to be mixing
With folk from the County, like you . . .

And your house! What a change from the Air Force,
All these huge full-length windows, so grand,
It's like something you see in the papers
And just *look* at your acres of land:

Do I "ride"? Oh you've got to be joking

How lovely to live such a lifestyle
And what a luxurious place,
– You're asking me if we like pheasant,
And if so, you'll send us a brace!

We've settled in, thank you for asking,
And how am I liking this life?
Let me tell you, it's been an "eye opener"
So far, as the new CO's wife:

You say that the aircraft are noisy
And some farmers complain, but not you?
Well, I'm sure that my husband's delighted
That you take it the way that you do . . .

How nice you've been wanting to meet us
To establish a thriving rapport
Like you had with a previous CO
(So *that*'s what this dinner was for!)

Do I "ride?" Oh you've got to be joking,
And I have to confess I don't "shoot"
– You must find me a great disappointment . . .
Not active in "County Pursuits",

So you've heard I'm a bit of a poet?
Yes, I write in the attic, it's true,
And if you keep on with these questions
I'll have plenty to write . . . about *you*!

Memory

(For Martin Ramsay, 6 March 1985)

I took a walk tonight
And dwelt
Upon the news today
Of Martin,
Who was far too young
To lose his life that way

I thought about
The pilots,
Brave young men
Who live their dreams . . .
Do they dwell
On danger
As they master their machines?

And who can know
The reason
For the scrambled scheme of things?
I only know
We lost a friend
Who flew those mighty wings

Now, when I look up
And see
A fighter, flying high,
A memory
Of Martin
Will linger
In
The sky

Farewell To The Wives

I can't believe I'm going
– Two years have simply flown,
It's such a wrench to say farewell
To all the wives I've known,

And being Wives Club President
Has been enormous fun,
For all the wives who've done so much
My thanks – to every one . . .

Living in the sticks up here
We need a club like ours
Where problems can be sorted out
And we can chat for hours,

We feel a "Kindred spirit" at these moments